P9-DCL-588

Written with Fire

Holt, Rinehart and Winston

New York · Chicago · San Francisco

Written
with Fire ⅄

THE STORY OF CATTLE BRANDS

EDNA HOFFMAN EVANS

Illustrated with Diagrams

Published, March, 1962
Second Printing, April, 1963
Third Printing, August, 1965

Grateful acknowledgment is made to Ludlow Music, Inc., New York, New York, for permission to use the words of "Whoopee Ti Yi Yo, Git Along, Little Dogies," collected, adapted, and arranged by John A. and Alan Lomax. Copyright 1938 by John A. and Alan Lomax in the book, COWBOY SONGS AND OTHER FRONTIER BALLADS. *Copyright assigned 1958 to Ludlow Music, Inc., New York, New York.*

Library of Congress Catalog Card Number: 62-8966

92593-0112
Printed in the United States of America

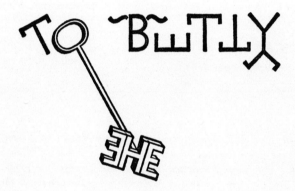

Contents

Written with Fire

1

Marks of the West

In the days when the West first became a cattleman's country, no barbed-wire fences or paved highways divided the land. The ranges were wide and open. They stretched for hundreds of miles, to the horizon and far beyond. There was nothing to stop a horse or a cow from galloping all day, or from wandering for weeks in any direction.

There were limits to the amount of land one man could claim, and cattlemen had to find some way of telling whose cows belonged on which range. Cows meant money in those days, just as they do today. No cattleman wanted to lose his livestock to somebody else.

The best way to identify a cow, pioneer Western cattlemen soon discovered, was to brand a mark on its hide. Once on, the brand lasted as long as the cow did. There was no way of taking it off. It could be changed, but a brand was a cattleman's mark of ownership, his way of saying, "Hands off. This cow critter belongs to me."

The cowboys made up a song with a verse that went:

Early in the springtime we'll round up the dogies,
Slap on their brands, and bob off their tails;
Round up our horses, load up the chuck wagon,
Then throw those dogies upon the trails.

When they sang these words they were describing one of their important jobs, that of marking the boss's cows for keeps.

Another important cowboy's job, mentioned in the song, was taking the herd up the trail, that is, taking it from open range to market. The cattle-driving trails crossed the Western country from Texas north to Wyoming, Montana, and the Dakotas; west to New Mexico, Arizona, California, and even as far as Oregon, and east to Kansas City. The cowboys took the herds

4

wherever there was a market for beef or a railroad to carry the cows to Eastern markets.

Trail driving was a big job for a few men on horses—never more than ten or fifteen men including the cook. There were extra horses to replace the worn-out ones, but there were no replacements for tired men. These few had to drive a herd of cattle numbering in the thousands across hundreds of miles of open country. Here again was a good reason for identifying the cows being driven; special trail brands were often added to the original markings just before the drive began.

Today, Western cattle ranches may cover thousands of acres—whole townships or more—but there are fences. Instead of the big drives, cattle are shipped to market by truck and by rail. Yet even today a rancher has to mark his cows. With steak selling at a dollar a pound or more and with hamburger not much less, every cow on the range means money in the bank later on.

It is not considered polite in today's West to ask a cattleman how many head of cattle he owns, for that is the same as asking him how many dollars are in his bank account. But ask him about his brand, and chances are he'll talk your ear off.

The brand designs chosen by early Westerners have continued to survive in today's West. A brand soon became a rancher's coat of arms, and he was proud of it. Not satisfied just to brand his livestock, the rancher marked his wagons, saddles, and all other ranch equipment with the same design. He often named his ranch after his brand. We can find many evidences of this in Western states today. It is impossible to drive anywhere in the cattle country without seeing signs that mark the Circle K ranch, the Lazy B, the Flying U, the Bar H Bar, the Seven T Six, and many more.

The West may not be as wild and woolly now as it was in the days of Buffalo Bill Cody and John Chisum. But as long as the West is cattle country, brand lingo will be the language of the range.

2

American Brands—
the Simple Ones

The people who settled along the Atlantic coast of
America in colonial times knew about branding. But
in those days the branding iron was used chiefly to
punish human beings. Runaway slaves were sometimes
branded when they were recaptured, and so were in-
dentured servants who tried to escape before their term
of service was up. People were also branded as punish-
ment for various crimes, but animals were not usually
marked this way.

It was not until American settlers began moving
west of the Mississippi, into the vast territory of Texas

and the Great Plains, that they felt the need for marking their cattle. Branding was already used for this purpose by the Spanish and Mexican ranchers who were settled both north and south of the Rio Grande. It did not take us long to adopt the same system.

The Spaniards and Mexicans liked elaborate brands, ones that were handsome designs, interesting to look at. The Americans were more practical. They wanted marks that could be put on quickly, read easily, and yet hard for a rustler to change.

To make his brands, the American cowboy took the alphabet and changed it around to suit his fancy. He changed the shapes and positions of the letters, and he made up new names for them. Besides the letters of the alphabet, the cowboy used three other basic sets of symbols. Thus, American brands are based on four different kinds of marks, used alone or in combination. They are:

1. Letters of the alphabet   3. Lines and circles
2. Numbers   4. Pictures

If a person can recognize and name these four different sets of symbols, he can read most American brands easily. There are some exceptions, of course, but generally all American brands follow this system.

Let's consider the letters of the alphabet. The American cowboy always uses capital letters when he makes up a brand. But in doing so, he uses lots of imagination and does things with the alphabet that no one else would think of doing.

To begin with, there are the regular letters. As brands they look quite normal, like this:

ABCE

HJKLSTU

But when the cowboy uses them, letters are apt to do strange things. They may tilt or tip backward or forward. When they do this in a brand design they are called tumbling, toppling, or tilting letters. They look like this:

The cowboy puts legs and feet on some letters and makes them appear to walk. Round or square-bottomed letters seldom walk, but some letters in the alphabet already have two legs, so all they need is feet. A few single-stemmed letters need the addition of both legs and feet before they can walk. Walking letters look like this:

AKN

JHYXR

Sometimes, instead of legs, the cowboy puts wings on some of his letters. These are called flying letters and they look like this:

AHMOUX

Running letters are formed in another way. In brand designs, instead of always using printed capital letters, the cowboy sometimes uses written capitals. These, written as you would write them on paper with a pencil or pen, are the running letters in brands. This is how they look:

$$MN$$

$$BYRa$$

The letters thus far have all been active ones. Some cowboy letters are just the opposite. Drag letters, for example, have a line that seems to be pulling or dragging them backward, like this:

$$AHK$$

$$MPRTXY$$

Least active of all are the lazy letters. These are the ones that lie flat or horizontal instead of standing erect. A lazy letter can lie face down or face up like this:

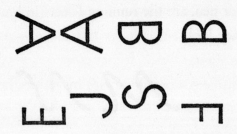

Finally, there are the crazy letters. These are the ones that are upside down, standing on their heads. Crazy letters look like this:

Not all the letters of the alphabet can be used in every one of these combinations. It would be pretty hard to make a tumbling O or a crazy X. C's are not very active, but a two-legged R can walk and it can run, and it can fly. Since E can be turned backward but not upside down, an inverted E is read reverse E rather than crazy E. An H cannot be crazy, because it looks the same upside down as it does right side up; but it can tumble and it can be lazy.

In the cowboy's alphabet, the letters O and I are not always read as letters. The O is often called a circle, while I can be read as the number one. I can neither tip nor be lazy—tipped, it looks like a slash, and lazy it looks like a bar.

What the cowboy does with his letters, he can also do with numbers.

There are walking numbers:

There are flying numbers:

There are drag numbers:

And there are lazy numbers:

There are also combinations of numbers joined in ways that only a cowboy's imagination could devise. Notice how the following number brands are made:

23   TWENTY-THREE   24   TWENTY-FOUR   33   THIRTY-THREE

44   FORTY-FOUR   46   FORTY-SIX   55   FIFTY-FIVE

57   FIFTY-SEVEN   63   SIXTY-THREE   74   SEVENTY-FOUR

76   SEVENTY-SIX   89   EIGHTY-NINE   96   NINETY-SIX

Sometimes, instead of registering a new brand for his young sons and daughters, a rancher will simply register his own brand with a number after it. Thus, if the family brand is A P B, there will be an A P B[1] for one child, an A P B[2] for another child, and so on, for as many cow-owning children as there are in the family.

3

More American Brands—
Lines and Circles

Lines and circles have definite meanings or readings when they appear in brand designs. Examine the following and see how they are named:

This is a bar. It is a short, horizontal line that can be used at the top or bottom or in the middle of a brand.

The rail is about twice as long as a bar. It is not used as often, and when it is used, it is apt to have letters sitting on or resting above it.

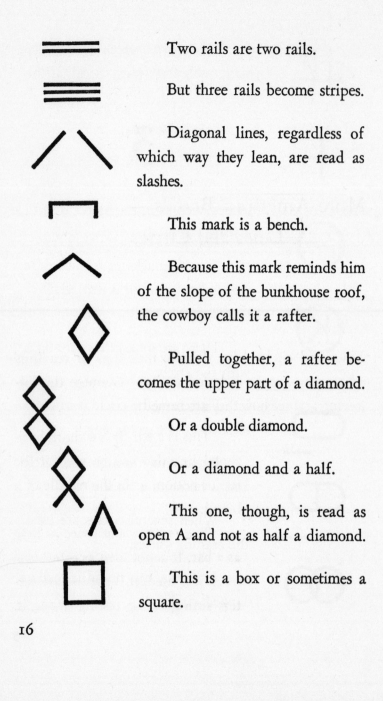

Two rails are two rails.

But three rails become stripes.

Diagonal lines, regardless of which way they lean, are read as slashes.

This mark is a bench.

Because this mark reminds him of the slope of the bunkhouse roof, the cowboy calls it a rafter.

Pulled together, a rafter becomes the upper part of a diamond.

Or a double diamond.

Or a diamond and a half.

This one, though, is read as open A and not as half a diamond.

This is a box or sometimes a square.

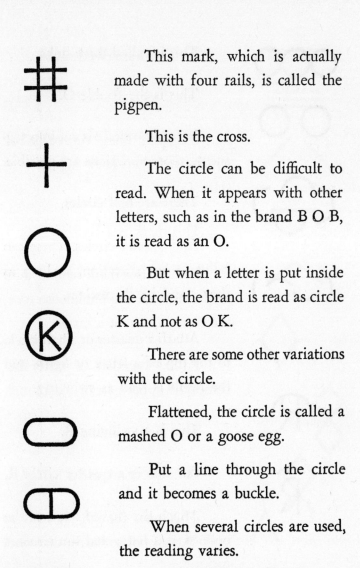

This mark, which is actually made with four rails, is called the pigpen.

This is the cross.

The circle can be difficult to read. When it appears with other letters, such as in the brand B O B, it is read as an O.

But when a letter is put inside the circle, the brand is read as circle K and not as O K.

There are some other variations with the circle.

Flattened, the circle is called a mashed O or a goose egg.

Put a line through the circle and it becomes a buckle.

When several circles are used, the reading varies.

In Texas, this brand is read as lapped circles.

 This is called three links.

This is the double O.

 When the circle is cut into segments, more variations are possible.

There are half circles.

 And quarter circles. These can point in any direction, so long as they stand by themselves.

 Attach a quarter or a half circle to the top of a letter or figure and the result is read as swinging.

This is a swinging R.

 But this is a quarter circle R.

Attach the curved mark to the bottom of a letter and the result is rocking.

 This is a rocking H.

This is also a rocking h, using a small letter. The brand is also read as the rocking chair.

 But this is H quarter circle.

A little distance, just an inch or so of space on a cow's hide, can make a big difference in the way a brand is read.

Brands are easy to read when a single symbol is used. For example, these can be recognized easily:

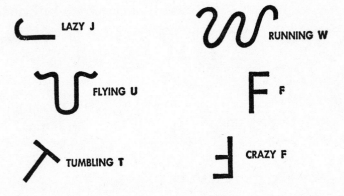

LAZY J

RUNNING W

FLYING U

F

TUMBLING T

CRAZY F

Usually, however, a brand design consists of two or more symbols. Many other brands have three different units in the design. Not many have more than three. After all, the space on a calf's hide is limited.

The same rules that are used in regular reading of the English language apply to the reading of more than one symbol. Always read the complete brand design:

1. From left to right.
2. From top to bottom.
3. From outside in.

To show how this is done, here are some brands and their readings:

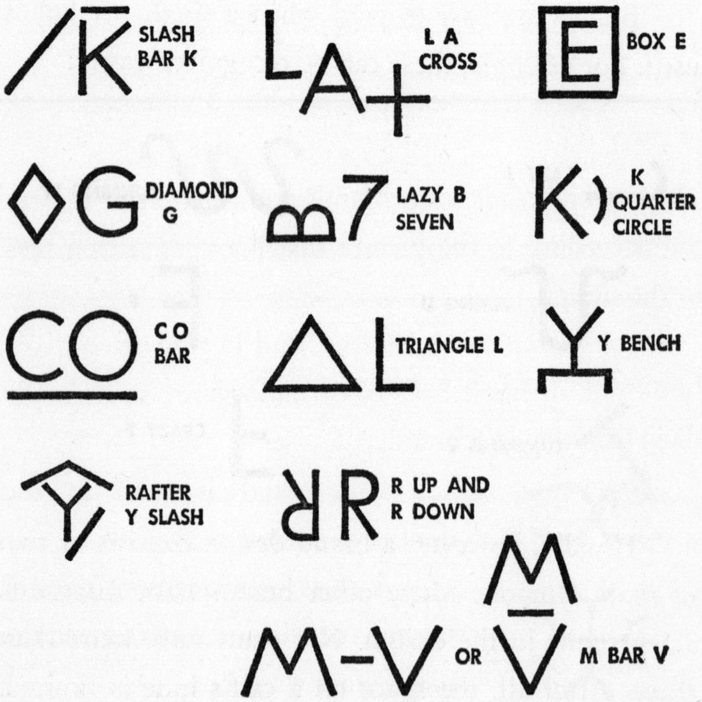
SLASH BAR K
L A CROSS
BOX E
DIAMOND G
LAZY B SEVEN
K QUARTER CIRCLE
C O BAR
TRIANGLE L
Y BENCH
RAFTER Y SLASH
R UP AND R DOWN
OR
M BAR V

4

Picture Brands

The cowboy reads some brands not as letters or figures but according to the picture that his imagination sees in the design.

For example, the letters C and U very often make him think of horseshoes or of mule shoes, so he reads them that way in a brand.

 This brand is read as the double horseshoe.

 A cross with quarter circles at the ends of all four arms is given the name cross wrenches.

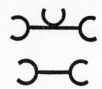

Three C's joined by a bar is not read as three C's bar, but as chain C.

Two C's joined by a bar can be read as C bar C, but it is also called the lazy wrench brand, because at some time or other it reminded some cowboy of that tool. And so the names go.

BOB ON THE SQUARE

DIAMOND TAIL

HOBBLED O

CROOKED H

CHAIN SEVEN

KID ON A RAIL

ALL THREE HAVE BEEN CALLED TURKEY TRACK

TURKEY FOOT

BAR MONEY DOWN

HORSESHOE A

DOUBLE T

KNOT ON A RAIL

BUZZARD ON A RAIL

NECKTIE

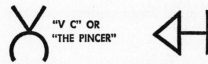 "V C" OR "THE PINCER"

 TRIANGLE H TRIANGLE

Sometimes, when the letters or symbols are joined together, the word connected is included in the reading. The following are samples of this practice:

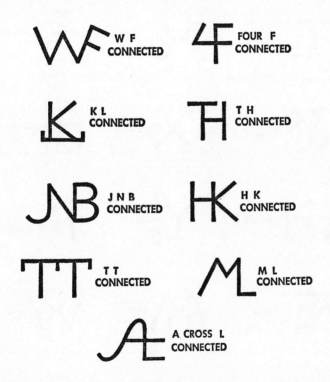

W F CONNECTED

FOUR F CONNECTED

K L CONNECTED

T H CONNECTED

J N B CONNECTED

H K CONNECTED

T T CONNECTED

M L CONNECTED

A CROSS L CONNECTED

But, often as not, the different symbols are run together and read as though they were separated by an inch or so of cow's hide. These are some that are not read as connected:

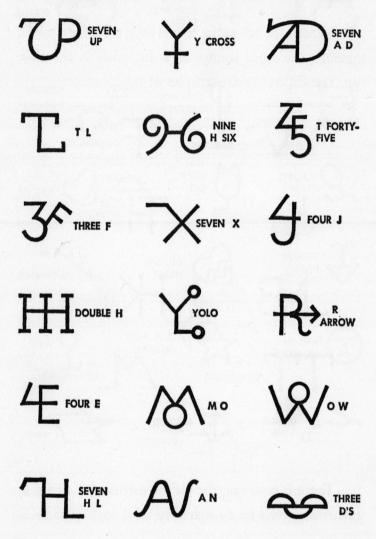

SEVEN UP

Y CROSS

SEVEN A D

T L

NINE H SIX

T FORTY-FIVE

THREE F

SEVEN X

FOUR J

DOUBLE H

YOLO

R ARROW

FOUR E

M O

O W

SEVEN H L

A N

THREE D'S

Finally, there are brands that are actual pictures.

STIRRUP

BOW AND ARROW

DOUBLE HEART

BRIDLE BIT

SAGUARO CACTUS

BROKEN SAGUARO

LAUREL LEAF

KITTY CAT

HAT OR SOMBRERO

FLOWER POT

BROKEN HEART

BUCKHORN

MAN IN THE MOON

STAR AND CRESCENT

WINE GLASS

GOURD VINE

ANCHOR

ANVIL

There is really no end to the cattleman's imagination when it comes to inventing and naming brands.

5

The History of Branding

The Spaniards and the Mexicans were not the inventors of branding. Being early settlers in the New World, the Spaniards brought the custom from Europe to Mexico. Later on, when American cattlemen settled in the West, they borrowed the idea of branding stock from their Spanish and Mexican neighbors to the south.

Nobody knows who first invented branding or when the custom began. It is an old, old practice, going back thousands of years. The ancient Egyptians used brands as marks of identification; so did the Babylonians, the Greeks, and the Romans. Not only animals, but slaves also were often branded with their owners' marks.

Before the arrival of the European settlers, there were no domesticated animals in North America except dogs. There were no cows or horses or sheep. The Western Indians hunted buffalo and mountain goats and bighorn sheep, but these were all wild creatures. The only animal to share the Indian's wigwam, hogan, or pueblo, and to accept him as master, was the dog— a half-wild creature probably descended from tamed wolves.

The Spanish Conquistadors brought the first horses to the New World. At first the Indians were frightened by the sight of a man on horseback. They thought the man and horse was a single creature. It was not until many years later, when the Indians learned to steal horses from the Spaniards or to capture the animals that escaped into the wilderness, that the Western Indians became such superb horsemen.

The Spaniards also brought the first cows and sheep. The first cows to arrive in Mexico were imported in 1521 by one of Cortes' followers. His name was Gregorio de Villalobos, and his herd consisted of one bull and six heifers—not a very big beginning for an industry that grew and grew until it spread from Mexico to the Pacific up to the Canadian border and as far east as Missouri and Kansas.

Along with these first cows and sheep, the Spaniards brought the first brands and branding irons to the New World. They probably learned the custom from the Moors, who brought it with them when they invaded Spain from Africa over a thousand years ago.

The first New World cowboys were Indians from Mexico, war captives enslaved by the Spanish conquerors. The Spaniards called them *vaqueros,* from the Spanish word *vaca,* meaning cow. Legend says that Cortes branded his Indian captives with the letter G for *guerra,* war. If so, the first cowboy probably had a brand mark on his own hide before he burned a mark onto the hide of the first calf born in Mexico.

On the cattle herds he owned in Mexico after the country was conquered and placed under Spanish rule, Cortes used a different mark. This was called the three Christian crosses, and it was just that: three crosses.

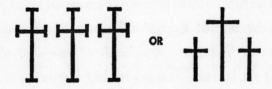

Sometimes the brand is shown with the crosses all the same size; sometimes it is shown with the middle cross larger than the other two.

Many of the very old Spanish brands are still in use on Mexican ranches today. Other, newer Mexican brands, modeled after those of Spanish ancestors, are also used. These Spanish and Mexican brands are quite different from those of the United States. As a rule, the Spanish brands are nice to look at, but they cannot be read. They have no names, except in a few cases where names have been invented for them.

There are some Spanish and Mexican brands on record in the United States. They are listed separately in a special section of brand record books kept by each of the cattle raising states.

Compare these Spanish and Mexican brands with the American brands shown in previous chapters.

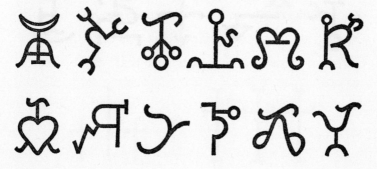

Today, many of the Western Indian tribes have become wealthy cattle owners. The tribal herds, which graze on the reservation ranges, are branded also. The brands used by the Indian cowmen are derived from tribal art and legend. They, too, have no popular English-language names. Like the Spanish and Mexican brands, many of the American Indian designs are beautiful and artistic.

The following are some used by the Navaho, Pima, Papago, and Apache tribes living in the American Southwest today.

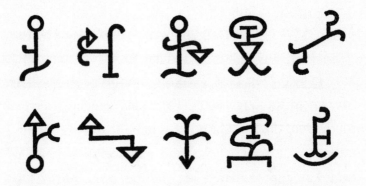

6

Spanish Brands with Stories

Many of the old Spanish brands have interesting stories.

The brand below belonged to a Mexican cattle king named Don Luis Terrazas, who lived in northern Mexico in the late 1800's. Don Luis' rancho stretched south from the Rio Grande for more than two hundred miles, and it extended east and west so far that its total area was approximately six million acres. On it Don Luis built five magnificent haciendas or ranch homes. He did this so that he could travel about over his land yet always have a comfortable place to stay.

The cattle on those millions of acres numbered more than four hundred thousand. It is said that once an American cattle buyer approached Don Luis Terrazas and said, "I would like to buy some cows, Don Luis. Could you sell me as many as four thousand head of three-year-olds?"

"Four thousand, señor," said Don Luis, smiling pleasantly. "Of course. Would you like to have them all the same color?"

Some people think they can see the initials T R S in the Terrazas brand. Old-timers who know Spanish brands say this is not so. The Terrazas brand, they say, was a handsome design—one that appealed to Don Luis' artistic senses—a design, nothing more.

Another Spanish brand with an amusing story belonged to Don Madariago Hipolito José del Castellana y Villaverde y Castro, who lived on a ranch in California in the days before it was a part of the United States.

Don Madariago looked at the rolling hills of his California rancho and designed a brand that resembled them. It looked like this:

One day some rustlers ran off with about a thousand head of the Don's cattle. They were busy re-branding the cows when Don Madariago and his vaqueros caught them.

When the Don saw what the rustlers had done to his brand, he was so angry that he turned the men over to a firing squad to be shot. The theft of his cows was bad enough, but the damage to his beautiful brand was unforgivable! By drawing a few extra lines with a running iron, they had transformed Don Madariago's three rolling hills into the face of a frog. This was the new brand:

There are a few exceptions, of course, to the no name custom of Spanish brands. The following are some of them.

This was called the arrow point, cross, half moon. It was owned by a rancher who lived on the Texas-Mexican border near Eagle Pass, Texas.

This brand is read JAV. It belonged to Juan Antonio Valli, a rancher who lived in Texas in the early days of its statehood.

José Antonio Navarro, a Texas patriot of Spanish descent, designed this JAN brand. Señor Navarro was one of the signers of the Texas Declaration of Independence in 1836. Later he was captured by the harsh Mexican general, Santa Anna, and held in prison for three-and-a-half years. The O at the top of Señor Navarro's brand is supposed to represent the iron ring in the prison wall to which he was chained during his years of captivity.

7

American Brands with Stories

Many American brands also have interesting stories. While the cattle owners north of the Rio Grande did not adopt the elaborate designs of their Spanish-American neighbors, they worked their own stories and experiences into their brands.

Shortly after the end of the American Civil War, a cattleman moved to Kaufman County in Texas. The war had taken most of his possessions. He had very little money and not much else besides his two .45 pistols and a few head of cattle. So he chose the 45 design as his brand, to show that his guns were in good working order. He also meant the brand as a warning to rustlers: he would shoot first and investigate after the smoke had cleared away.

Another Texas brand was originally called the flying half circle, diamond and a half, but that took too long to say. Besides, not everyone could recognize it.

 One day a new cow hand rode in, stared at the brand on the hide of a steer, and scratched his head. Then he muttered, "That sure looks like the Fleur de Mustard to me." And so the brand got a new name.

Out in northern Arizona in the 1880's a ranch that stretched for ninety miles north and south and forty miles east and west used a brand that looked like this. What it was originally called has long since been for-

 gotten. But to the cowboys who worked on the ranch, the brand looked like the tool used by the chuck-wagon cook to chop up the meat and vegetables that went into the hash. So the brand was named hashknife, and the ranch and all hands on it were known as the Hashknife Outfit. The

Hashknife Outfit no longer exists, but the hashknife brand is still used in Arizona.

Another Arizona brand, which is still important today, was named by five brothers in honor of their home town back East. The Babbitt brothers—David, William, Charles, George, and Edward—got tired of running a grocery store in Cincinnati, Ohio. The West called them, and in 1886 they moved to Flagstaff, Arizona, bought a herd of cattle, acquired land and water rights, and became cattlemen. For a brand design they chose C O bar—C for Cincinnati and O for Ohio—their old home town. The C O bar Cattle Company puts its brand on many new calves at round-up time each year; sons and grandsons of the original five brothers operate the business.

Brand designs are chosen for many reasons. A Texas ranchman, with a romantic heart, used the number 70 as his brand because he was married in the year 1870.

Brands change, too. The wine glass H brand was run in Texas as long as alcoholic liquor was sold in the ranch's home county. But in the year 1896, the county went dry—that meant no more beer, wine, or whiskey for thirsty cowboys. To show that it was a law-abiding place, the ranch turned its brand upside down (no more wine), and changed the reading from wine glass H to H wine glass.

There are some brands that not even a cowboy can read. But that does not keep him from giving them a name. In Texas, a brand design made up of two half circles facing each other slightly off center was unreadable until some cowboy came up with a bright idea. "Let's call it the *quien sabe,*" he suggested. And

 quien sabe, which means who knows in Spanish, is what the brand has been called ever since.

 The *quien sabe* brand also exists in Arizona, but it is different from its Texas cousin. In Arizona, the who knows brand is three quarter circles in pyramid form.

The King Ranch in Texas, which is the largest working ranch in the United States today, uses a

running W as its brand. Mexican vaqueros employed on the ranch call the brand the little snake, and it is not hard to see why.

The running W is a brand that is known and respected wherever cattlemen gather. One time a King Ranch outfit was on a drive through Nebraska, a long way from home, and short of cash. The trail boss needed money to pay off some cowboys who had been fired for getting drunk on the job, so he went to the bank in the nearest town and tried to cash a check.

"You look all right and you talk all right," the banker said, "but can't you give me some identification?"

"Do you know the King Ranch brand?" the trail boss asked.

The banker admitted that he did.

The trail boss climbed on his horse and spurred off toward camp. Before long he was back, calling for the banker to come out. Strung out behind him along the town's dusty main street was his "identification."

"Look," he told the banker when the latter stepped outside. "Here are a hundred and fifty saddle horses branded running W. Our chuck wagon and the mules pulling it, the saddles my men are sitting on, and even the pies the cook just baked have the same brand. If that isn't enough identification, I have fifty-six hundred steers herded up about three miles outside town, and they've every one of 'em got a running W on their ribs."

The banker laughed. "I'll bet I'm the only banker in the world who has ever been offered this kind of identification," he said. "Get off that horse and come in and write your check."

Another big Texas ranch used XIT as its brand. There are several different stories told about the origin of that design. One of them is that XIT stood for Ten in Texas, because the owner's ranch covered ten counties. It only covered nine, but ten made a better story.

The tale most often given as the true origin of the brand is that the ranch foreman thought awhile, and then drew the brand design in the dust with the heel of his boot. "There's your brand,"  he told the owner, who was known as Colonel "Barbecue" Campbell. "You can make it with five slaps of a bar iron, and no rustler can work it."

Colonel Campbell liked the design and promptly adopted it. But one clever rustler did manage to change the XIT brand, as will be described in another chapter.

8

How Brands Are Registered

"You may have three million acres of ground and a lot of cows, but you ain't got a ranch till you get a brand and burn it in the hides of your cows." That is what one Texas cowboy had to say about the importance of brands.

Anybody can design a brand. Anybody can have a branding iron made with that design on it—any blacksmith, welder, or iron worker can do the job. But not everybody can register a brand and make it legal.

How do you register a brand?

First, and most important of all, a person must

own livestock—cows, horses, or sheep—to put the brand on. Without animals to wear the brand, there is no point in cluttering up the brand record books with a lot of unused designs.

With that one all-important point taken care of, the rest of the process is simple. The next step is to design a brand. This done, you must go to the brand registration office and fill out a brand application. In most states, brand records are kept by the Live Stock and Sanitary Board or by the State Department of Agriculture.

On the brand application you must tell on what kind of animals you are going to use the brand, and where you are going to put it on the animal. There are a number of possibilities: the jaw, neck, shoulder, ribs, hip, or thigh; either on the left or the right side. Location of the brand is usually different for cattle and for horses. Sheep are either fire branded with a hot iron on the nose or the brand is applied with paint or tar on their wool.

The brand clerk examines a new design. First, he makes sure that it is not like any brand already registered. Next, he checks to see whether the new brand could easily be changed into someone else's brand.

After a design is approved by the brand clerk it is published in the state cattleman's bulletin. This is done so that any other brand owner may object, if he thinks the new brand is too much like his own. If no one objects, the new brand is accepted and becomes the legal possession of the person in whose name it is registered.

In order to keep their brand records up to date, many states require re-registration every ten years. This way, brands that are no longer used do not clutter up the records. But as long as a rancher keeps his brand alive and on record, it is his rightful possession and no one else can use it.

Registered brands can be sold, just like any other piece of property. The transactions are recorded as carefully as the deeds to real estate or documents that indicate ownership of other valuable possessions.

If a brand owner dies, his brand is transferred to his heirs in the same way and with the same legal procedures as are used in handling his other forms of property. A brand is every bit as important in the eyes of the law as are land, cattle, or machinery.

Are there many brands on record?

Indeed there are. Every state that has a cattle industry also has a large brand registration. To give a few figures: Arizona has more than 13,000 different brands on record; Wyoming has more than 25,000; New Mexico has nearly 26,000; Colorado has more than 36,000; and Montana has more than 63,000. Even the State of Florida, which is not a Western state, but which does have a thriving cattle business, has more than 10,000 brands on record.

Texas, the cattle-raising granddaddy of them all, does not have a statewide brand registry. Texas has had laws requiring the registration of brands ever since 1848, but brands are registered by county and not by the state as a whole. Each of the 254 counties in Texas has its own brand registration system. It has been estimated, however, that there are more than 500,000 cattle brands in use in Texas.

Ear marks are just what the name says. They are slits or notches cut in a cow's ear, either left or right, or both, like this:

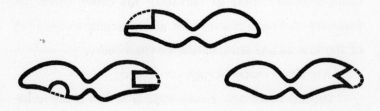

At the same time that he registers his brand, the cattleman can also register ear marks. These are optional, but most ranchers use them as additional marks of identification.

Some cowboys claim they can read ear marks at a greater distance than they can brands. But it takes sharp eyes and the right amount of know-how to do either one, especially when the light is dim or the air is full of dust.

It is not hard to see why brand registration is necessary, or why cattlemen have gotten together and worked for brand registration laws. By the enforcement of these laws, and by the employment of brand inspectors who check cattle on the open range and at shipping points and central markets, the activities of rustlers and cattle thieves have been brought under control.

9

Cowboy Writing

Branding hurts calves, but not as much as one might think. No burn, not even a small one that scarcely raises a blister, is pleasant. So the calves bellow and squall, and run to their mothers who sympathize with them and comfort them. Before long, the pain and fright are forgotten, and the calf is as happy and healthy as ever.

It takes skill to do a good job of branding, and it takes several tools. Old-time cowboys used fewer tools than modern ones do, but the modern ones probably do a better, quicker job.

There are several different kinds of branding irons.

One is a stamp iron. This iron has the brand design worked out in metal (in reverse, of course), which is attached to a long iron handle.

To make a complete brand of several different symbols, several stamp irons may be used. Some stamp irons are pictured here.

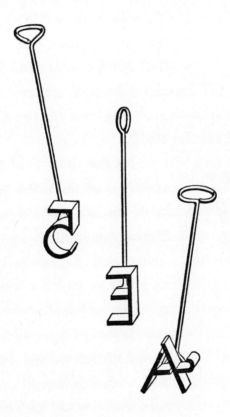

Another iron, similar to the stamp iron and often used in connection with it, is the bar iron. This is simply a narrow piece of iron set at the end of a handle. Used once, it makes a bar or a slash mark. Used several times (the cowboy describes the process as "socking it on") the bar iron can make letters and symbols like the square and the bench.

The XIT brand, for example, was made with five applications of the bar iron, two for the X, one for the I, and two for the T.

Another iron, used by honest ranchers and also highly favored by cattle rustlers, is the running iron. This is merely a long iron rod with a curve or hook at one end. The running iron is used like a hot pencil, to "draw" a brand on the hide of a calf. Some old-time cowboys maintained that they could write better with a running iron on a cow's hide than with pen and ink on paper.

Rustlers liked the running iron because it was easy to carry. Often they had it made in two sections, so that it could be taken apart and hidden in a saddlebag when it was not in use. Mere possession of a running iron was not considered good evidence against a man—without seeing it in action, no one could say for sure which brand it might have drawn. But because it was such a handy tool for rustlers, the running iron has been outlawed in some states.

The old-time cowboy did not need either a stamp iron or a running iron to do a good job of branding. All he needed was a brass or iron ring that could be carried in his pocket or tied to his saddle string. When a cowboy found a calf that needed branding, he built a small fire, cut a couple of green sticks from a nearby bush, and using crossed sticks as handles went to work. He quickly drew on the brand with the hot metal ring.

Some brands can be traced directly to these rings. For example, there is the hip O brand and the ring bone. Both of these are merely circles burned on the hide of the hip or around the protruding hip joint. They are also examples of two different names used to describe a brand consisting of a single circle.

In the old days cattlemen used much larger brands than they do today. The long rail used by John Chisum was a single line that ran from the shoulder to the hip. Another large brand was the rail under tail, which was another line running from the hip around the rear of the animal, under the tail, to the other hip. The saddle

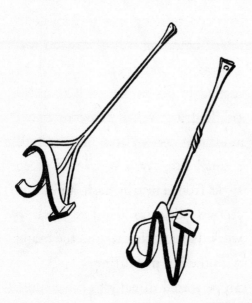

MEXICAN STAMP IRONS; NOTE THE SHORTER HANDLES AND MORE COMPLICATED DESIGNS.

THIS SHOWS THE COMPARITIVE
SIZE OF MEXICAN AND AMERICAN
(CENTER) IRONS. THE MEXICAN
IRONS HAVE A HOLLOW END SO A
WOODEN HANDLE CAN BE INSERTED
FOR GREATER LENGTH. THE AMERI-
CAN IRON IS THREE FEET LONG.

AMERICAN STAMP IRONS; NOTE THE
LONG HANDLES.

THEY READ:

H, T BAR L, HORSESHOE, BAR T FIVE, AND Y SLASH.

pockets brand consisted of a large diamond on each hip connected by a line across the cow's back.

These large brands went out of favor when leather from cow hide became valuable. A brand spoiled the quality of the leather and cut down its selling price.

Present-day brands are seldom more than three inches high when first applied to a calf's hide. But the brand grows as the calf grows, so that a three-inch brand can be a foot high when the cow is four years old.

Modern times and modern conveniences have found their way to the range, as they have to all other parts of the country. Old-time cowboys would laugh at it, but the latest thing in branding technique is the electric branding iron. It can be plugged in wherever there is current, and in less than two minutes the brand design is glowing hot and ready.

These electric irons cost more than the old-fashioned stamp irons, but they are supposed to do a better job and make a clearer brand, because the heat can be controlled and kept constant.

Another modern improvement in branding tools is the butane furnace that can be used in place of the old-fashioned bonfire to heat the stamp irons. This, too, gives better control of heating. Some modern stamp irons are made of copper, because that metal holds a more even heat for a longer time than iron does.

A good job of branding does not require an iron as hot as one might think, and the hot iron is not left on the hide very long. The idea is to burn through the hair and into the hide, but *not* through the hide. A properly burned brand will peel in a week or so, and hair grows over the scar in such a way (it stands up higher or lies in a different direction) that the mark is always visible.

If the iron is too hot, or if it is left on too long, the brand will blotch—that is, the lines will run together, and after it heals the mark will be hard to read. Too deep a burn may not heal properly, and it is much more apt to get infected with the dreaded screwworm. To prevent this, the modern rancher uses medication along with his branding iron to clean the burn and to keep the flies away.

Some ranchers prefer to burn their brands with acid rather than with heat. But acid burns will blotch and smear more easily than heat brands. For this reason, unless they are applied with a steady hand, they are not too satisfactory. The old hot-iron brands are still considered the best.

These are branding don'ts that every good cattle-man keeps in mind at branding time:

DON'T *try to brand with anything but a hot iron; you can't freeze on a brand with a cold iron, but . . .*

DON'T *let the iron get too hot; it starts a hair fire and usually results in a poor brand.*

DON'T *use a forge or a gas fire carelessly; it heats the iron too quickly and can "burn up" any iron. Wood makes the safest fuel for branding fires.*

DON'T *try to brand wet animals; dampness will cause a brand to scald, resulting in a blotched brand.*

DON'T *be in a hurry; take your time. The animal will wear the brand all its life, so give it a good one.*

DON'T *get tender-hearted; the iron must burn deeply enough to remove hair and the outer layer of skin. When the iron is lifted, the brand should be the color of saddle leather.*

What the cows think of branding has never been written. But since millions of them have worn brands, and still do, the practice can't be any worse than many other treatments that humans and animals get during the course of their lives.

10

Roundup Time

Roundup is the time when most of the branding is done, and roundups come in spring and fall. Spring is the most important time, for it is then that all the calves born on the range are rounded up, along with their mothers, and their owner's mark put on them.

In the days of the open range, before barbed-wire fences (the cowboy calls them bob-wire), roundups were even more important than they are today.

Several ranch outfits would usually work together, riding systematically over an area and driving all the cattle into a central location or corral. The old cows already wore their owner's brand, and it was a fairly simple matter to mark a calf with the same brand as its mother's.

Very seldom did the range cows have twins, although rustlers often tried to make it appear that way. And when a calf wearing one brand was seen following a cow wearing another brand—well, somebody had some fast explaining to do.

When all the cattle were corralled, the branding crews built their fires and heated their branding irons. Often there would be several different brands being used at the same time, and it was the job of the roper at the corral to notice what calf belonged to what cow.

The roper was a mounted cowhand who worked out of the corral. He caught the calves, lassoing the little ones around the neck and leading them to the branding crew. Larger calves were heeled—that is, roped by the heels and dragged to the place where the rastlers were waiting.

When the calf came within his reach, the rastler leaned over the animal's back and grabbed two handfuls of skin, one handful near the flank and the other near the foreleg. Holding on, he leaned back and flipped the calf over on its side. Before the surprised and upset calf could object, the rastler caught hold of its top foreleg and got a knee on its neck to hold it down. His partner caught the top hind leg and pulled it straight out behind, bracing his foot against it for further control.

With its hide thus stretched, the calf was branded and ear marked. It was then released and allowed to scramble to its feet. Of course, it lost no time in galloping back to its mother, bawling at the top of its voice. Soon mother's soft, moist nose reassured the youngster, and her tongue licked the hurt from the burned spot. In a surprisingly short time the misery and fright were apparently forgotten.

The branding crews worked hard all day, making sure no calf was left without an identifying mark. Then, if there were still more open range to cover, the roundup crew moved on and the process was repeated when a new crop of cows and calves had been collected.

Occasionally, when he was riding the range, a cowboy came upon an unbranded calf. When this happened, he quickly unlimbered his rope and caught the stray. Then he built a small fire and went to work, usually using a running iron or a branding ring that he carried in his saddle bag or had tied to his saddle.

Today, roundups are not the elaborate cross-country affairs that they once were. Ranches are fenced now, but even so, when a ranch extends over thousands of acres, it is no small job to round up the cows and see that the calves are all branded.

Most ranches now have regularly established and permanent corrals. These consist of a complicated series of pens, with one or more narrow chutes connecting them. In these permanent corrals you are apt to find a squeeze chute at a narrow place in one of the runways. This device does away with roping and rastling.

Instead of being roped and led or dragged, the calf is urged into the chute and then blocked front and rear. Movable sides are pushed together and the animal is squeezed between them and held motionless. All it can do is bawl its protests. It cannot move in any direction. While in the squeeze chute, the calf can be branded and worked on more easily than if it were stretched out on the ground with a man tugging at either end.

Modern ranch practice has made the branding time more complicated. The calf may be de-horned, and vaccinated against the disease called blackleg. Other medication is also given to prevent infection, especially screwworm. A medication called Smear EQ 335, which was developed by the United States Department of Agriculture, is the one most often used.

The squeeze chute is often used with horses, as well as with cows. Horses are more high strung, and the treatment recommended for them is gentler than that given cows. Horse brands are smaller, too, and are more often put on the shoulder than on the flank.

Old-time cattlemen preferred to put their brands on the left side, for some reason or other, and as near the cow's tail as possible. They said that brands within reach of the cow's "fly knocker" were less apt to get infected, because the cow could switch her tail and keep the flies away while the brand was healing.

Nowadays, because of the vast numbers of brands in use, some of which are bound to be similar but placed on different parts of the animal's body, a brand is as likely to be on the right side as on the left; and on the neck, shoulder, or ribs instead of the hip.

Fall roundups are not as big as the spring ones, but they, too, are necessary, especially if the herd is to be moved from summer pasture to winter feeding pens. Yet whether it comes in spring or fall, roundup is a busy, hard-working time on the range.

11

Mr. Maverick's Brand

When a cowboy sings:

Whoopie ti yi yo,
Git along, little dogies . . .

he is singing about orphaned calves or calves that have
become separated from their mothers. Naturally, without the old cow to look after them, these youngsters
are apt to be thin and scrawny. The term dogie origi-
nated in Texas, but just why or how nobody seems to
know for sure.

When a cowboy talks about a maverick, on the

other hand, he is using a term that can be traced to one man—a Texas lawyer named Samuel A. Maverick.

Mr. Maverick lived in Texas in the days when that part of the country was trying to win its independence from Mexico. Sam Maverick was a lawyer and politician, and he was also one of the men who risked their necks by signing the Lone Star State's Declaration of Independence in 1836.

Lawyer Maverick was much more interested in politics, legal matters, and land speculation than he was in the cattle business. However, one of his clients was short of cash, so instead of paying Mr. Maverick for his legal services with money, the client settled the fee with four hundred head of cattle.

These cows were allowed to run loose on a small island just off the Texas coast in the Gulf of Mexico. Mr. Maverick hired a cowboy to look after the animals. Part of the cowhand's job was to put the lawyer's brand, MK connected, on the new calves. But the cowboy was inclined to be lazy. Besides, the cows could not get off the island, and all the cows on the island belonged to Sam Maverick. So why bother to brand them?

After the Republic of Texas became a part of the United States of America and the Mexican War was over, Mr. Maverick ordered his herd moved to the mainland. The lawyer assumed that his rancher neighbors would know that all unbranded cows and calves found on the range were Maverick's. But an unbranded cow was like a loose ten dollar bill. Before long, the Maverick stock was wearing brands other than the MK connected.

Use of the word maverick spread across range country. Its meaning changed with the years. At first a maverick was any unbranded yearling calf. Later, it came to mean anything—animal or man—that was astray or wild or unclaimed or without any definite ties or loyalties.

A maverick brand was an unrecorded brand, but even an unrecorded brand, in theory, could keep an animal from being driven off the range along with regularly branded stock. Still, in case the ownership of a maverick-branded animal was questioned, there was no way of proving just who was its rightful owner.

The best thing to do with a maverick, cowmen soon discovered, was to put a registered brand on it as soon as possible. In a way, mavericking came to be a mild term for stealing. A maverick on the open range, as the custom went in Texas, soon belonged to the man with the longest loop and the fastest horse.

So, even though he was not particularly interested in the cattle business, Samuel A. Maverick's name has become a permanent part of the language of the range.

12

Rustlers at Work

"I picked this brand because I figured a rustler would have a hard time changing it into any other brand." That is how many old-time ranchers explain their brand designs.

It was a simple matter to put a brand on an unmarked calf. It was harder to take a brand already on a cow and "work" it into some other design. But many a rustler rode the range looking for somebody else's cows; and when he found them, he often did a pretty good job of brand working then and there.

The rustler did not need much working equipment. His favorite tool was a running iron, but he didn't even need that. A piece of telegraph wire would do just as well. The wire could be bent and twisted into any shape. Heated in a small fire, it could then be run into an old brand in such a way that the alteration would be very hard to detect. When not in use, the wire was easily hidden—more easily, even, than a running iron.

Besides drawing additional lines, there were other ways of changing brands. Some rustlers put a piece of wet blanket over the old brand on a cow's hide and then applied a red-hot frying pan, scalding off all the hair around the branded area. In a month or so, when the hair grew back, covering the marks of the original brand, a new one could be put on over it.

Dishonesty at branding time also "paid off." The man who used the branding iron could merely hair brand a calf—that is, he could singe the hair but not burn the brand deeply enough to make a permanent scar. Then, when the singed hair grew out, a new brand could be put on without any other mark showing.

Once a rustler had made his new mark and the brand had healed, the alteration was often hard to detect. If the work was well done—and it took some

65

skill to work a brand properly—the only sure way to detect a change was to kill the animal in question and skin it. The older brand showed up much more clearly on the flesh side of the hide than the newer marking did.

Sometimes a line or two was all that a rustler had to make in order to change a brand. Sometimes the job was more complicated. Here are some original brands, along with the new brands that rustlers worked them into.

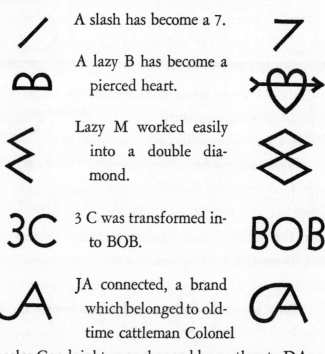

A slash has become a 7.

A lazy B has become a pierced heart.

Lazy M worked easily into a double diamond.

3 C was transformed into BOB.

JA connected, a brand which belonged to old-time cattleman Colonel Charles Goodnight, was changed by rustlers to DA.

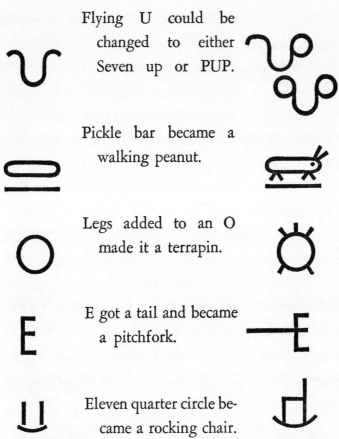

Flying U could be changed to either Seven up or PUP.

Pickle bar became a walking peanut.

Legs added to an O made it a terrapin.

E got a tail and became a pitchfork.

Eleven quarter circle became a rocking chair.

One cattleman in early Arizona studied the brands used by four of his neighbors. They were:

After some thought and figuring, he went to town and

registered his own brand. It looked like this. After that, whenever he found a cow belonging to any of his neighbors he got busy with his running iron and did a little work. He had built up quite a large herd before the vigilantes caught up with him.

To prove a charge of rustling, it was usually necessary to catch a man in the act of changing a brand. But there were other ways of detection, too. Sometimes, when a rancher suspected that rustlers were at work in his vicinity, he would leave some "markers" to catch them. Markers were calves with some peculiar color or marking that could be recognized easily. These calves were left unbranded. Then, if they turned up later wearing some other brand, the owner could quickly recognize and claim them.

One time the Arizona Rangers suspected a man of rustling and brand-changing, but they were never able to catch him at work. So they chose several ordinary-looking calves, cut a small slit in the hide of their necks, and inserted a silver half dollar in each of the slits. Later, when the calves turned up at the loading corral wearing the suspected man's brand, all the Rangers had to do was feel the coins in the animals' necks and they had all the proof that they needed.

Another rancher, this one a Texan, used an IC brand. A rustler with a sense of humor added another letter, and the brand became ICU. But the original owner had a sense of humor, too. He also had enough ranch hands to round up the stolen cows and change the brand once again. When the cowboys were finished with their branding irons this time, the cows were all wearing a brand that read:

$$\frac{ICU}{2} \text{ (I see you, too)}.$$

The most famous brand working job of all was the one done on the XIT brand in Texas. Colonel "Barbecue" Campbell thought he had a brand that could not be tampered with. But a clever rustler went to work with his running iron and proved that Colonel Campbell was wrong.

The rustler noticed that the top of the T in the XIT brand was often slanting; this was because of the way the calf's hide was stretched when it was rastled down at branding time. On brands with T's that did slant, the rustler had no difficulty at all in changing the XIT to the star cross brand. It is said that Colonel

Campbell finally paid the rustler five thousand dollars in cash to show him how the brand was changed.

This is the way the rustler did it:

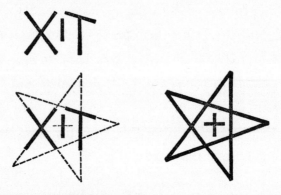

Today, the problem of cattle rustling is still a big one in the cattle country. Brand inspectors are employed by all the ranching states to check brands at shipping centers and at central markets.

But with highways cutting across the ranges, and with covered trucks that can travel fast at night, rustlers do not bother so much about changing brands any more. Instead, they kill the cows, skin the carcasses, and dress the meat at some secluded place on the range. The beef is loaded into refrigerated trucks, and even though the branded hides may be left behind as evidence, who can prove what brand a steak or a pot roast wore when it roamed the range on its own four legs?

13

Well-known People
and Their Brands

Down through the years a number of important and well-known people have owned cattle brands.

Hernando Cortes, the conqueror of Mexico, was the first European to place his brand—the three Christian crosses—on cattle in the New World. His Spanish followers were not slow in doing the same thing with cattle and brands of their own.

Not long after Cortes became master of Mexico, another Spaniard made his mark in the New World. His name was Álvar Nuñez Cabeza de Vaca—*cabeza de vaca* means head of a cow in Spanish. One of Álvar

Nuñez' ancestors had won the name by helping the King of Spain in his war against the Moors. This ancestor followed a band of raiding Moors and marked an important point in the trail with a cow's skull. When the King followed and defeated the raiders, he made the tracker a knight and gave him a name of honor—Cabeza de Vaca—in memory of his clever and courageous action.

Álvar Nuñez Cabeza de Vaca was the first European to see the Great Plains and grazing lands of the American Southwest. Shipwrecked after an expedition to Florida, he walked all the way from the eastern coast of Texas, across New Mexico, into Arizona, and down into old Mexico to the Spanish settlements there.

 His descendants, many of whom live in the Southwest today, have changed the spelling of the name to De Baca, but they still use the ancient family brand design. Burned on the hide of a cow, the De Baca brand looks like this.

Another Spanish brand that is well known in Texas was owned by Stephen F. Austin, the man who most deserves the title of the "Father of Texas."

Austin organized and led the first group of American colonists who settled in Texas when that region was still a part of Mexico. He was a leader in the struggle to gain independence for Texas; he was a statesman, soldier, and cattleman. His brand looked like this. It had no name and no reading. In Austin's time, as today, the design was known simply as Stephen Austin's Spanish brand.

John Chisum, who was one of the cattle kings of Texas and New Mexico, used the long rail as his brand. This was a single line burned along the left side of a cow from the shoulder to the tail. Instead of taking its name from the brand, as was usually the custom, Chisum's outfit was known as the Jingle Bob, because of the ear mark he used. This mark was made by slitting the ears of each cow lengthwise, so that the lower halves would hang down loosely along the animal's face, forming the so-called jingle bob.

John Blocker was a cattleman who drove some of the largest herds up the trail from Texas to Kansas. In the year 1882, he reported that he had fifty-one thousand two-year-old cows on the trail. Blocker's ranch

73

brand was APB, but when a cattle drive was organized, each animal received a new brand, a trail brand. John Blocker's trail brand was an inverted seven, placed on the left shoulder of cows and on the left hip of cow ponies.

Most trail brands, like John Blocker's, were small and simple. They were placed high on an animal's back, neck, or jaw, so that they could be seen easily from horseback by the cowboys driving the herd. It was not easy to keep track of thousands of cattle in the long drives, but an easy-to-see trail brand helped.

Some cattlemen used their names or initials as brands; others got their nicknames from the brands they used. Colonel B.H. Campbell, boss of the XIT ranch, got his nickname that way. Before the XIT brand was created or his Texas ranch was organized, Colonel Campbell was branding cattle in the Kansas-Indian Territory with a brand that read bar BQ. It looked like this. Before long, the initials B.H. were forgotten, and Colonel Campbell was known forever after as "Barbecue."

Theodore Roosevelt was interested in ranching

long before he organized his Rough Riders to fight in the Spanish-American War in Cuba and before he became president of the United States. As a boy, Theodore Roosevelt had been rather sickly. Later, when he was a young man just out of college, he set out to prove that he was as strong and tough as the next fellow. He chose to do this by roughing it in the West.

At first, young Teddy Roosevelt's neighbors, and the cowboys in the North Dakota Badlands ranch country, were not too sure about the young dude. Teddy had funny Eastern ways; he had big teeth that showed whenever he grinned his wide grin, and he wore thick glasses. Besides all that, in the excitement of a roundup he would shout, "Hasten forward quickly there!" instead of just plain, "Hurry up!"

But Teddy Roosevelt had a way with him, and he soon won a place in Western hearts. 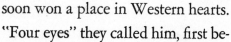 "Four eyes" they called him, first behind his back, and finally as a sign of friendship to his face. He had two ranches and three brands: the elkhorn, the triangle, and the Maltese cross. Teddy Roosevelt's Maltese cross brand is still an active one in North Dakota today.

In the 1920's, when Edward, the Duke of Windsor, was the young, dashing, and horse-loving Prince of Wales, he owned a ranch in western Canada. As a basis

for his brand design he used three ostrich plumes. These plumes have been on the coat of arms of the heir to the English throne since the days of the knightly Black Prince, back in the fourteenth century. The brand was called the three feathers and it looked like this. Cowboys on the Prince's ranch used it on the right shoulder of his horses. Another brand, EP for Edward Prince, was used on the cows' ribs.

The late cowboy humorist, Will Rogers, used several brands on cattle raised on his ranch in Oklahoma. His own personal brand was called the dog iron, be-

cause it looked like an old-fashioned andiron or firedog. Will Rogers also continued the brands used by his father, CV on cattle and J4 on horses.

Today, Stewart Granger, the movie actor, has three brands registered for the cattle and ranch he owns in southern Arizona. They are the 7K quarter circle, the

⅄ K NAN ᕫᗡ

NAN, and a design that seems to defy description until one looks at it carefully. Then it is easy to see that it is made up of the letters TFG, which were initials of the man from whom Granger bought it.

C.W. "Pinky" Gist, the well-known rodeo clown, uses two Y's—one lazy and the other crazy.

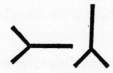

And to end the list—which could go on and on—Roy Rogers, the "King of the Cowboys," uses his initials as a brand design. It looks like this:

14

Funny Brands and Fancy Ones

While brands and branding are serious business in ranch country, the cowboy enjoys a laugh too well to pass up any chances for humor. Sometimes he even makes jokes with his brand designs.

There is the story of the two hungry cowboys who came upon a chuck wagon out on the range. The cook was off somewhere, but the food was ready. The two cowboys ate their fill and then, with a running iron from one of their saddlebags, they left a message for the cook branded on the seat of his extra pair of pants. What was the message? It read simply WE8—we ate.

Before the cook returned, a third hungry cowpoke came along and helped himself. Then he added another brand to the cook's pants. His brand read ME2—me too.

When the cook did get back to his chuck wagon, he did not care about the food that had been eaten. But the brands his uninvited guests had put on his extra pants made him angry. So he climbed back on his horse and set out after the jokers. When he found their camp, he added his own brand to their extra gear. This gave him the last laugh and showed what he thought of the jokers. The brand he used was YY, and the cowboys knew, when they read it, that the cook thought they were too wise for their own good.

Some ranchers have had fun designing their brands and making jokes at the same time. For example, there are brands that read:

IMᵐ I AM LAZY E   IMИ I AM LAZY TOO

IGO I GO   IGO2 I GO TOO

Modern dude ranches, designed to please vacationing Easterners who spend their holidays out West, use fancy eye-catching and ear-charming brand names. Probably the brands are never burned on many animals, just on the ranch remuda stock intended for the Easterners to ride. But they sound fine, and look pretty good, too.

All the following are registered brands out West.

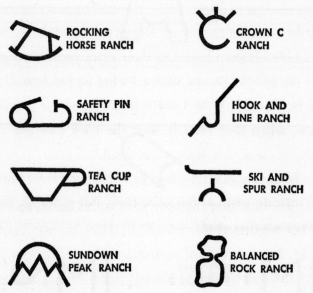

ROCKING HORSE RANCH

CROWN C RANCH

SAFETY PIN RANCH

HOOK AND LINE RANCH

TEA CUP RANCH

SKI AND SPUR RANCH

SUNDOWN PEAK RANCH

BALANCED ROCK RANCH

Not all fancy brands are designed for the tourist trade. Some serious cattle companies use similar ideas. There are, for example:

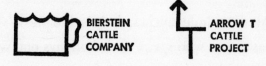

BIERSTEIN CATTLE COMPANY

ARROW T CATTLE PROJECT

No one can say that Western ranchers do not keep up with the times, even in the rocket and space age.

While no one knows for sure what a flying saucer looks like, or whether such things exist, one rancher went ahead and registered a flying saucer brand. It looks like this:

Another rancher uses a rocket as his brand, and all his animals wear a mark like this:

To show that anything goes on his dude ranch, the owner registered this brand: Ō. How do you read it? Why, bar nothing, of course.

In order to remind himself that his ranch and cattle are a long way from being paid for, one cattleman registered an MA brand. He explains to his friends that the letters stand for Mortgage Acres, and his acres certainly are.

15

Design Your Own Brand

Old-time cowboys, it is said, used to amuse themselves around the campfire, after the day's work was over, inventing new brand designs that could not be changed by rustlers. They would draw the designs on the ground, using a stick for a pencil. One cowhand would draw his design, and then the others would try to work it into something else.

Some present-day ranch owners design their own brands; others buy brands already registered and active. To register a new brand, as has already been said, a person must own livestock on which to use it.

But there are many unregistered brand designs used in a variety of ways. They may serve as monograms on stationery, on shirt pockets, neckties, or on other possessions and articles of clothing. They can be printed on letter-heads, embroidered on cloth, stamped or burned on leather. They are sure to create interest wherever they are used.

How does one go about designing his own brand? The same methods of procedure used in the Old West still hold true today. The best brand is a simple brand. It should be easy to read and easy to apply. A good brand is one that will not blotch—that is, it will not smear and the lines will not run together, no matter whether it is printed on paper, stamped on cloth, or burned on a cow's hide.

The best brands are open ones—that is, they do not have small corners or fine details; not too much is crowded into a small space; there are no closely drawn lines or figures to blotch or run together.

Brand letters are always in capitals; good squared-off letters are the most favored. The exception comes when running letters are used; they are capital letters in script.

Most brands do not exceed three characters,

whether these are letters, numbers, curved or straight lines of one kind or another, or pictures.

There are exceptions to the three-symbol rule, of course. Some well-known brands consist of a single letter or figure; these are usually quite old. Some brands consist of two or more connected symbols that can be drawn as an unbroken line. A few brands have more than three characters, like the USIS brand used by the United States Indian Service. But these are the exceptions, rather than the rules.

A person's initials can easily be worked into a brand design. Many cattlemen have used their own initials, or the initials of their wives, sons, or even their home towns. For example, the author's initials, EHE, can be worked into any number of combinations:

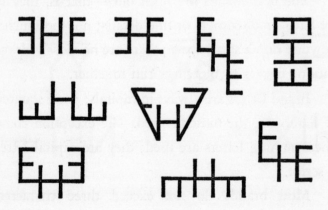

Any set of initials can be worked the same way.

Some people have names that can be made into picture brands, or which can be read from a very few symbols. Some of these are:

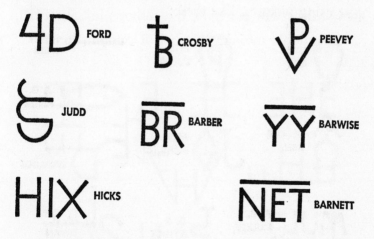

Some ranchers have used all the letters of their

last names, but in such a way that the name makes a design rather than a signature. For example:

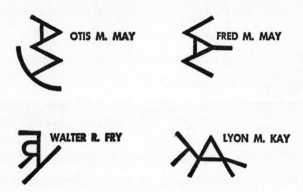

OTIS M. MAY

FRED M. MAY

WALTER R. FRY

LYON M. KAY

Note: The names must be short.

Other ranchers have made picture brands of their names, either by combining letters and pictures or by just using pictures, like these:

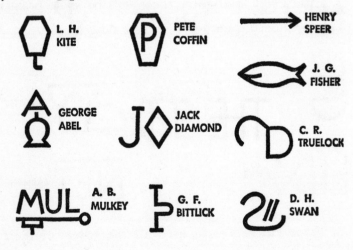

L. H.
KITE

PETE
COFFIN

HENRY
SPEER

J. G.
FISHER

GEORGE
ABEL

JACK
DIAMOND

C. R.
TRUELOCK

A. B.
MULKEY

G. F.
BITTLICK

D. H.
SWAN

With all the letters in the alphabet and all the numbers, plus quarter circles, half circles, diamonds, bars, rails, and rafters; with lazy letters and crazy letters; with running, walking, and flying letters; with drags and swings and rockers; with pictures of almost everything from anchors to rockets; there are almost endless combinations that can be made into brand designs. Even though thousands of brands are already registered and worn by millions of cattle on the range today, the possibilities are by no means exhausted.

The cowboy can still sing:

Early in the springtime we'll round up the dogies,
Slap on their brands, and bob off their tails. . . .

And every springtime there will be some brands that are, indeed, brand new on the range.

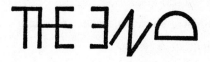

About the author

EDNA HOFFMAN EVANS' interest in brands and branding began when she moved to Arizona in 1948. She found her first branding iron in a secondhand store; her collection of irons from Texas, Old and New Mexico, Canada, and Florida now numbers close to fifty, and several of them were used as models for the sketches in *Written with Fire*.

After receiving both a B.A. and an M.A. from Florida State University, Miss Evans worked for several Florida newspapers, including the *Times* of St. Petersburg, where she grew up. She was photography editor of *Nature Magazine* for fourteen years, and still contributes a number of articles to Western and natural-history periodicals. The author of three books for children, she now teaches Children's Literature at Phoenix College in Arizona.